DEAR READER,

WELCOME TO KOOB, THE BACKWARDS BOOK.
YOU NEED TO THINK UPSIDE DOWN AND
TИOЯꟻ OT ꓘƆA𐐒 WHEN DOING THESE ACTIVITIES.
SO GET YOUR BRAIN IN GEAR, AND START
BY WRITING THIS MESSAGE WITH YOUR
LEFT HAND IF YOU'RE RIGHT HANDED AND
YOUR RIGHT HAND IF YOU'RE LEFT HANDED:

I PROMISE TO THINK BACKWARDS
WHEN USING THIS KOOB.

--- --- --- --- --- --- --- ---

--- --- --- --- --- --- --- ---

--- --- --- --- --- --- --- ---

SIGNED: --- --- --- --- --- --- ---

(I HOPE YOU SIGNED YOUR NAME BACKWARDS)

DECODE THESE INSTRUCTIONS WITH A MIRROR.

1. FIND A BASEBALL HAT AND WEAR IT BACKWARDS.

2. PUT YOUR SHIRT ON BACK TO FRONT.

3. PULL YOUR PANTS ON THE WRONG WAY.

4. TELL A FAMILY MEMBER THE WIND CHANGED WHEN YOU WERE GETTING DRESSED AND NOW YOU'RE STUCK LIKE THIS!

HOLD A PENCIL BETWEEN YOUR
TOES
AND DRAW A PICTURE
ON THIS PAGE.

WRITE A *SECRET* MESSAGE AND THEN...

①

②

③

GLUE

THESE TWO PAGES TOGETHER.

Write the alphabet backwards, and draw the letters backwards, too!

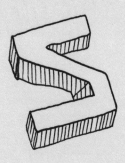

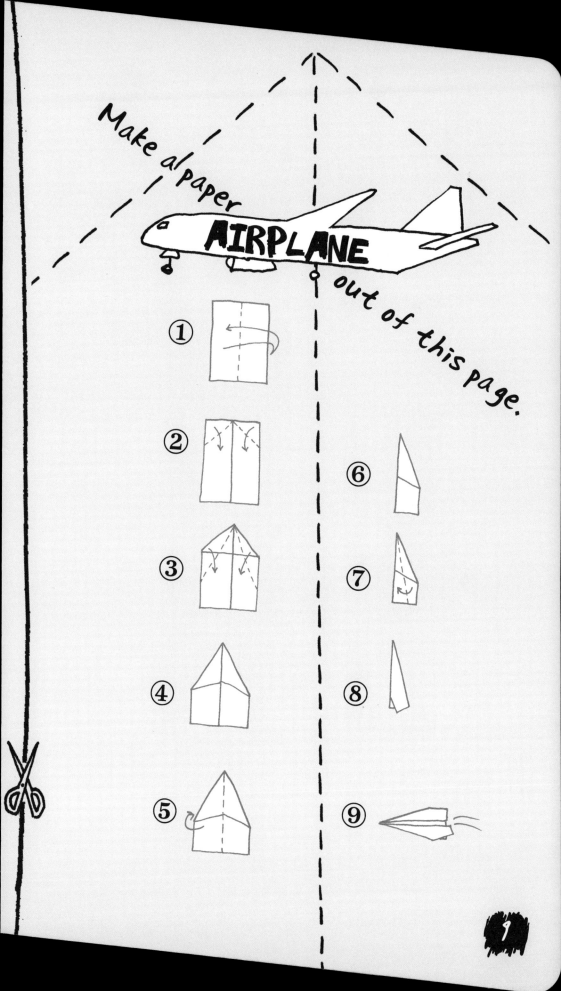

Make a paper **AIRPLANE** out of this page.

① ② ③ ④ ⑤ ⑥ ⑦ ⑧ ⑨

7

CAN YOU READ THIS  WRITING?

GOOD JOB. YOU CAN READ THIS! DID YOU USE A MAGNIFYING GLASS? NOW TRY TO WRITE THIS SMALL.

This rainbow is upside down and made up of unusual colors. What are they?

What's at the
beginning of the
rainbow?

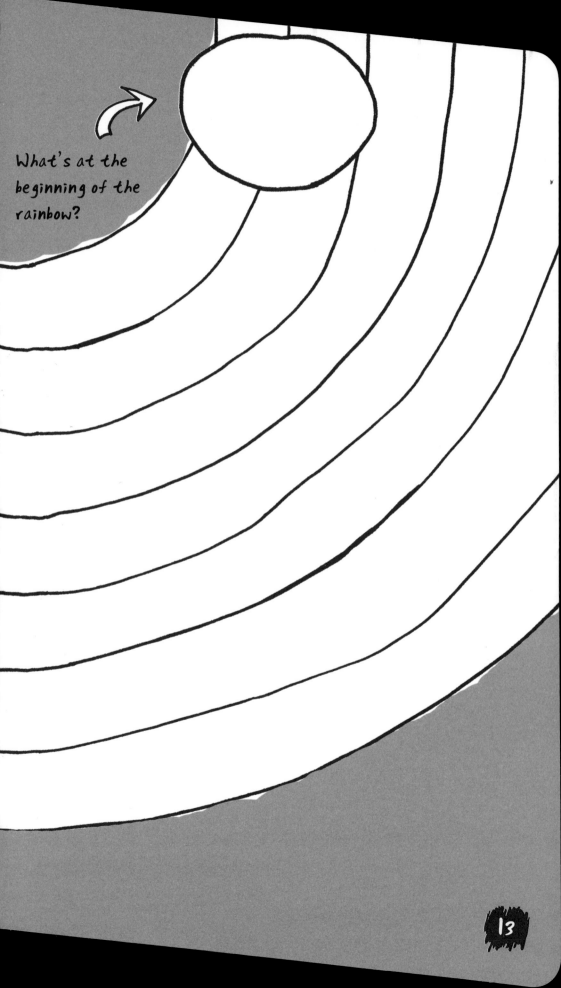

PUT SOME PEANUT BUTTER OR JELLY ON

14

YOUR LIPS AND THEN TAKE IT OFF BY FILLING THESE PAGES WITH KISSES.

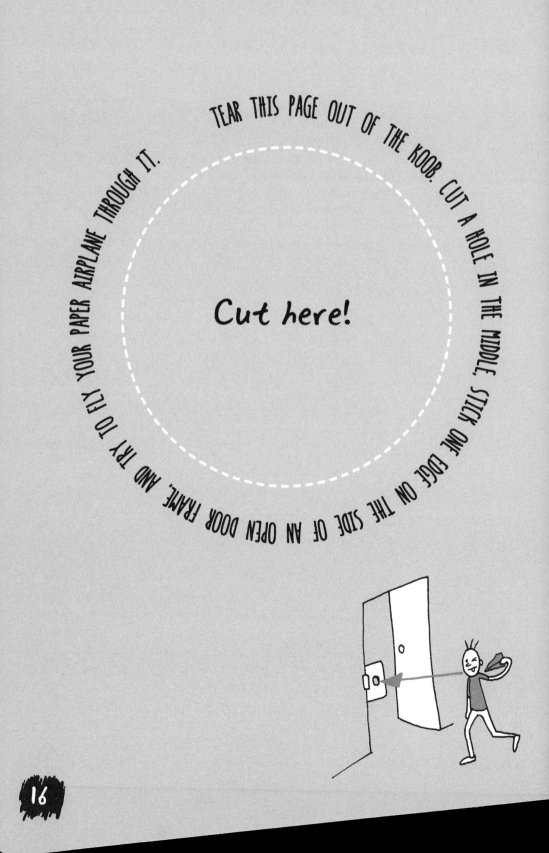

TEAR THIS PAGE OUT OF THE KOOB. CUT A HOLE IN THE MIDDLE. STICK ONE EDGE ON THE SIDE OF AN OPEN DOOR FRAME, AND TRY TO FLY YOUR PAPER AIRPLANE THROUGH IT.

Cut here!

Color this page...

...but remember to think backwards, so leave the page blank and color the edges instead.

Combine two of your favorite fruits to make a brand new fruit. Give each new fruit a name, then draw them here.

Example: an appange!

19

Give these objects some texture by holding the pages over a tree trunk and coloring them in against the tree.

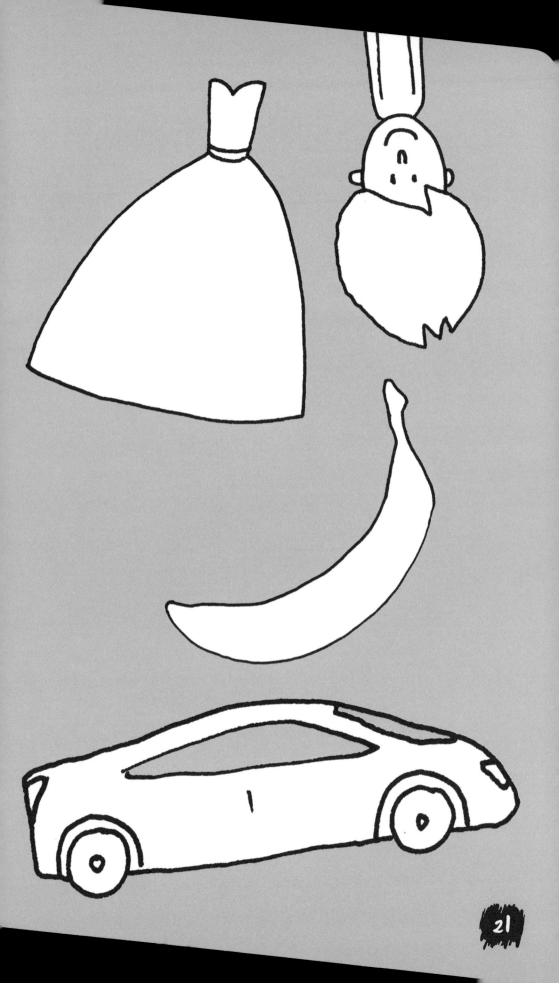

DRAW A LARGE DOT USING
SMALL DOTS.

COUNT HOW MANY DOTS YOU DREW:

NOW CONNECT ALL THE DOTS TOGETHER.

CUT OUT THESE DINOS AND
HOLD ON TO THEM FOR LATER.

Stick your T. rex on this page so it looks like he's biting this person's head off! Then color him in.

DRAW OR STICK A PHOTO OF YOUR FACE OR YOUR FRIENDS' FACES IN THESE HEADS.

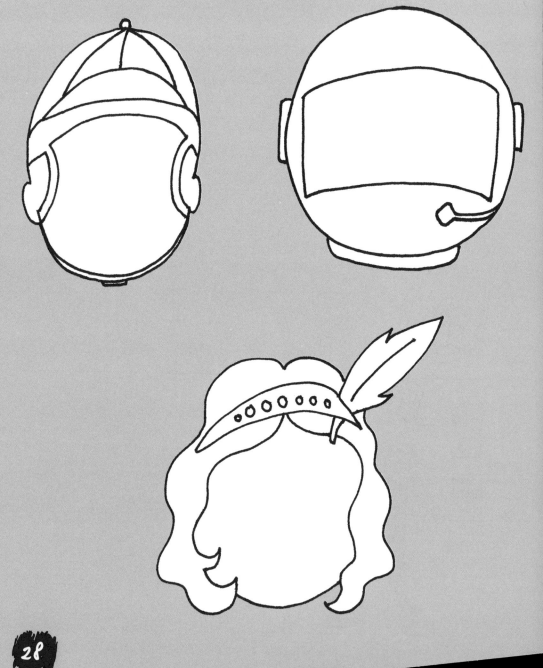

① ----------

② ----------

③ ----------

④ ----------

DEFINITELY DON'T
DO THIS ONE!

⑤ -----------------------------

⑥ -----------------------------

⑦ -----------------------------

TIME HOW LONG IT TAKES YOU TO DRAW THIS VASE OF FLOWERS THREE TIMES.

NOW TAPE THREE DIFFERENT PENCILS TOGETHER
AND TIME HOW LONG IT TAKES YOU TO DRAW
THE SAME VASE THREE TIMES.

HAVE YOUR
STEGOSAURUS
FROM PAGE 25 TEAR THROUGH AND
"TAKE A BITE" OUT OF THE NEXT PAGE.

GLUE SHADED AREA

CREATE "DINOSAUR SKIN" ON THIS PAGE BY GLUING DOWN PIECES OF ONION SKIN, ORANGE PEEL, OR OLD LEAVES.

THEN TURN BACK TO THE PREVIOUS PAGE AND GLUE IT ON TOP OF THE "SKIN" TO CREATE YOUR 3D STEGOSAURUS.

GLUE SHADED AREA

There are four giant letters on pages 38-41. Figure out what word they spell and write it here:

. . . .

Clue: remember to think upside down and back to front.

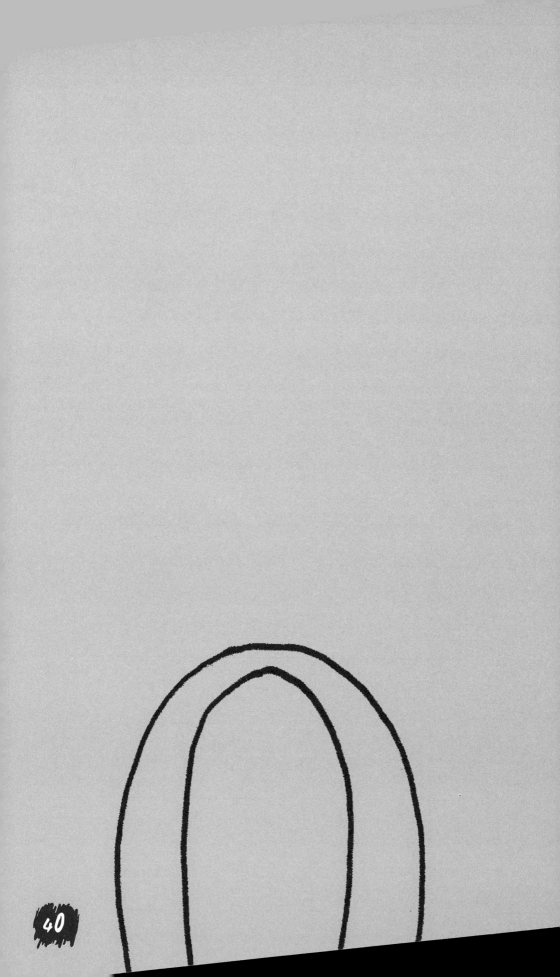

40

UNBAKE THIS CAKE BY DRAWING THE DIFFERENT INGREDIENTS THAT WENT INTO IT.

BUTTER

....

....

....

....

....

....

①

②

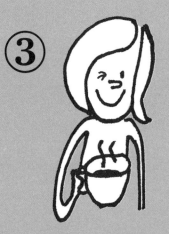

③

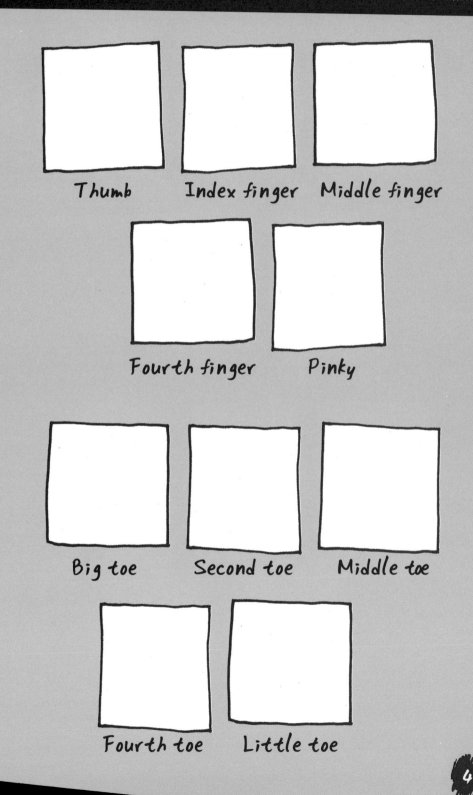

MAKE REVERSE FINGERPRINTS BY DIPPING YOUR FINGERNAILS IN PAINT AND PRESSING THEM ONTO THE PAGE. COMPARE THEM TO YOUR TOENAIL PRINTS.

Thumb

Index finger

Middle finger

Fourth finger

Pinky

Big toe

Second toe

Middle toe

Fourth toe

Little toe

Grab a pencil and use it to fill these pages with scribbles. Then use an eraser to draw new pictures within the scribbles by erasing some of the pencil marks.

REDRAW THE
COVER OF THIS
KOOB AS IF IT WERE
A REGULAR BOOK
AND NOT A
BACKWARDS BOOK.

52

53

COVER THESE PAGES IN CLEAR TAPE, WRITE ON THEM WITH DRY-ERASE MARKERS, THEN WIPE THEM CLEAN.

55

Cut out this
shape, then turn
the page.

58

Stick a picture of you wearing your clothes backwards on page 56. Then tape this picture frame around it.

1. Place the koob behind you.

2. Get a mirror and hold it out in front of you so you can see the koob.

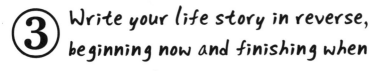

③ Write your life story in reverse, beginning now and finishing when you were born.

STAPLE THESE TWO PAGES
TOGETHER.

Use a white pencil to draw stars in the sky.

⭐ Make some · · constellations.

DRAW A SCENE ON THIS PAGE AND THEN CUT OUT THE JIGSAW PUZZLE PIECES. STICK THE PIECES BACK INTO THE KOOB IN THE WRONG PLACES.

71

72

STICK YOUR MIXED-UP PUZZLE PIECES HERE.

WRITE YOUR AND
YOUR FAMILY'S NAMES

!SDRAWKCAB

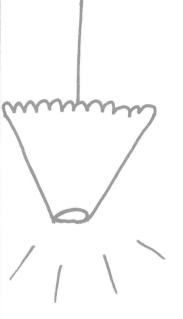

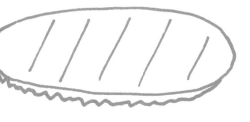

USE MASKING TAPE TO CREATE SHAPES ON THIS PAGE. THEN PAINT OVER EVERYTHING USING AS MANY COLORS AS YOU WANT. WHEN THE PAINT HAS DRIED, PEEL OFF THE MASKING TAPE. PRESENT YOUR MASTERPIECE AS A WORK OF MODERN ART.

79

What comes out must go in.

HOW MANY **PALINDROMES**
CAN YOU WRITE HERE?

(REMEMBER: A PALINDROME IS A WORD OR PHRASE THAT READS THE SAME FORWARDS AND BACKWARDS.)

Cover these pages in *glitter!*

Now try to get every single
piece of glitter off the page.

DRAW AN ANIMAL ON THE OPPOSITE PAGE AND CUT IT OUT. THEN, ATTACH A PIECE OF STRING TO IT AND TAKE IT FOR A WALK!

DRAW SOMETHING WITH YOUR FINGERNAIL.

TIP: PRESS DOWN HARD TO MAKE INDENTS ON THE PAGE.

USE AN ERASER TO
ERASE
THIS DOT.
KEEP GOING UNTIL
YOU'VE RUBBED
A HOLE THROUGH
THE PAGE!

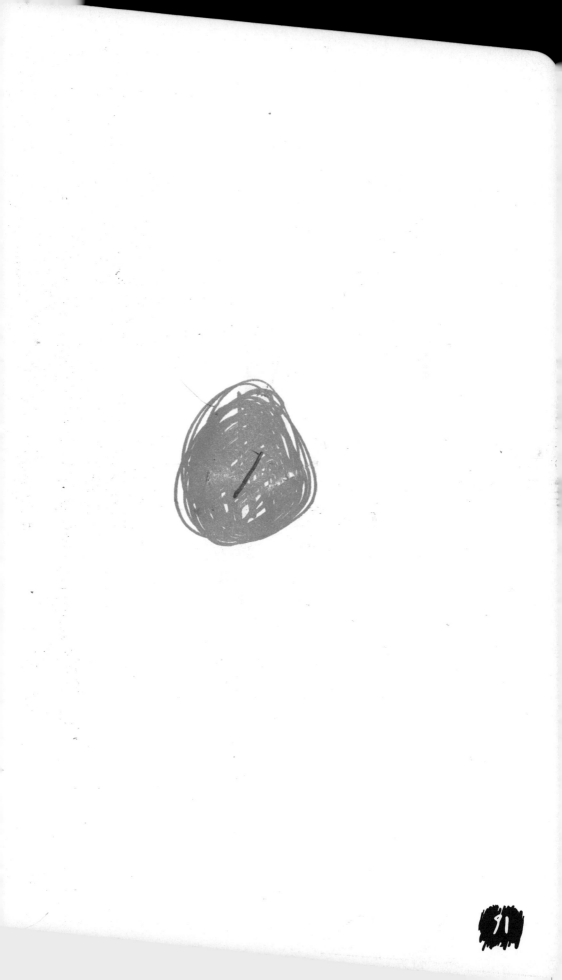

GET AN ANIMAL TO MAKE A

PAW PRINT

ON THIS PAGE.

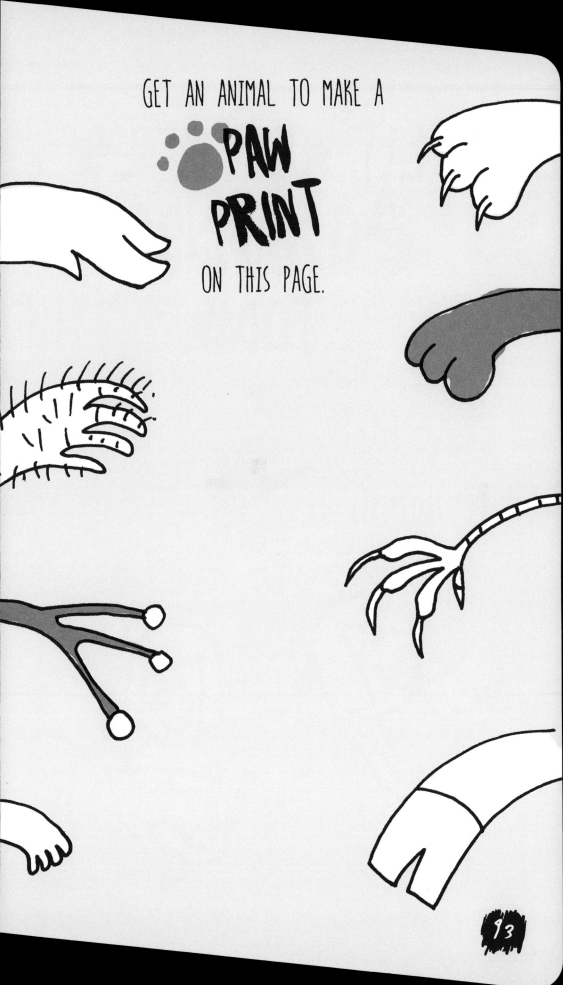

EAT YOUR MEALS BACKWARDS TODAY.

BREAKFAST:
START BY SLURPING MILK OUT OF
YOUR BOWL, THEN EAT DRY CEREAL.

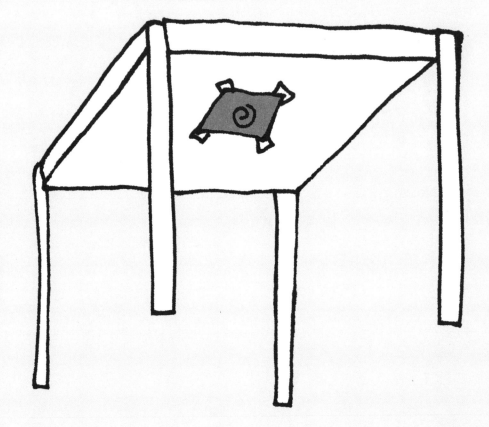

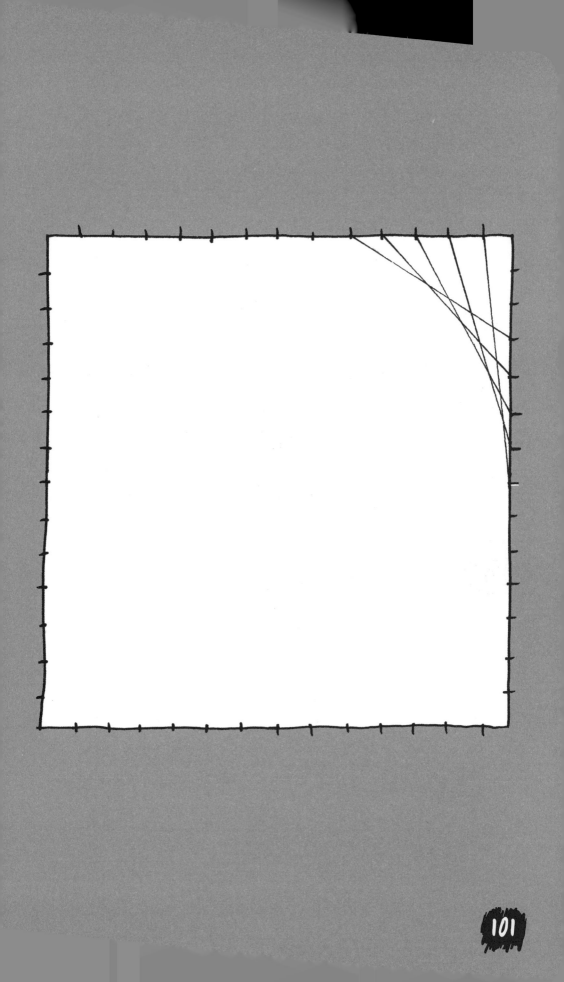

WEAVE THIS PAGE

USING PAPER FROM PAGE 105.

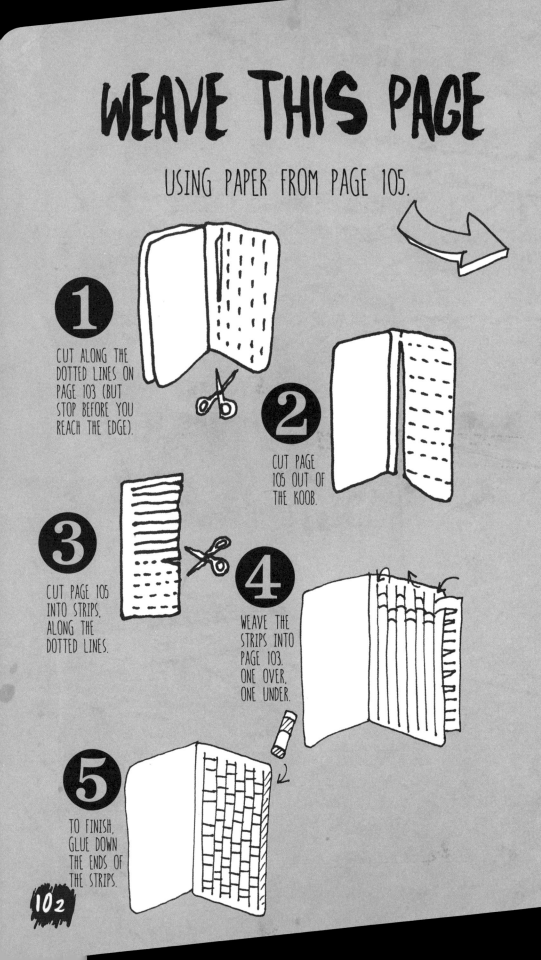

1 CUT ALONG THE DOTTED LINES ON PAGE 103 (BUT STOP BEFORE YOU REACH THE EDGE).

2 CUT PAGE 105 OUT OF THE KOOB.

3 CUT PAGE 105 INTO STRIPS, ALONG THE DOTTED LINES.

4 WEAVE THE STRIPS INTO PAGE 103. ONE OVER, ONE UNDER.

5 TO FINISH, GLUE DOWN THE ENDS OF THE STRIPS.

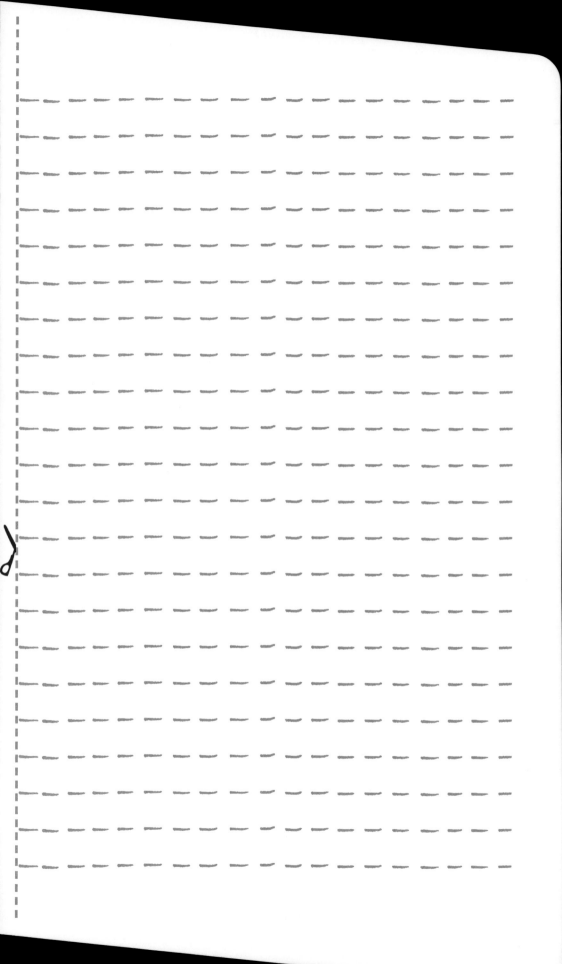

BEARD OR HAIR?

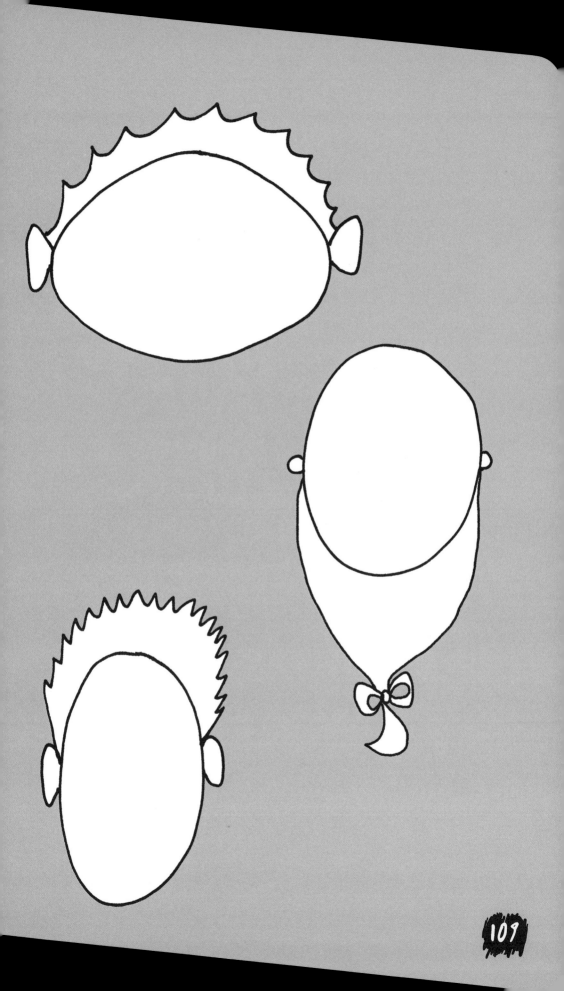

Draw
a
self-portrait
without
taking
your pen off
the page.

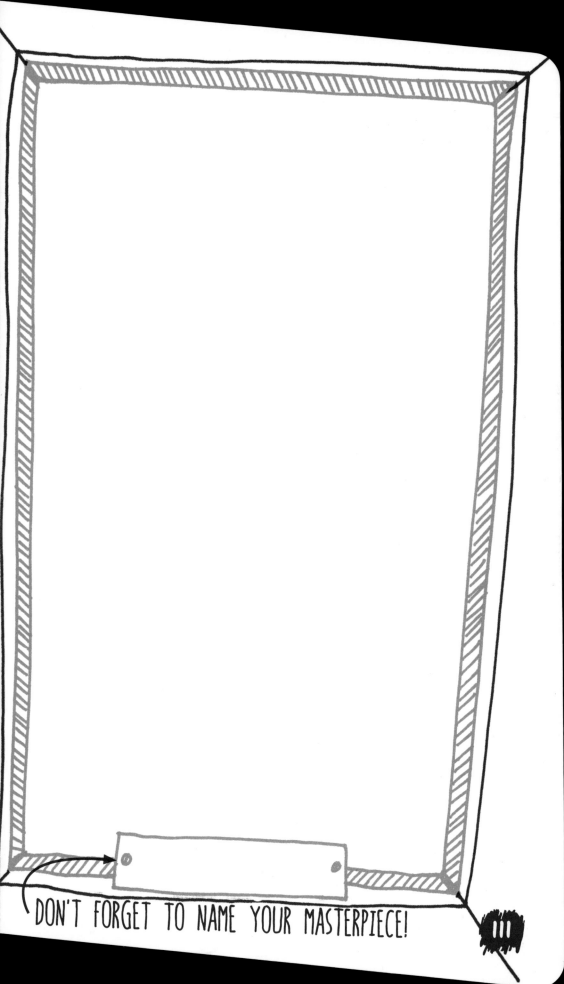

DON'T FORGET TO NAME YOUR MASTERPIECE!

What did you dream about last night?
Draw it in the cloud.

113

DRAW YOUR HOUSE BY UNFOLDING AND TAPING

PAPER CLIPS TO THE NEXT PAGE TO MAKE LINES.

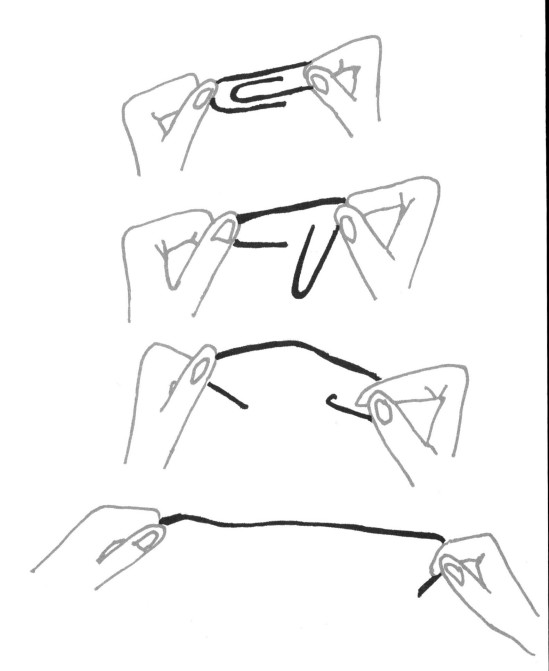

SQUEEZE SOME LEMON JUICE INTO A BOWL AND ADD A FEW DROPS OF WATER. DIP A COTTON SWAB INTO THE MIXTURE AND WRITE A SECRET MESSAGE ON THE NEXT PAGE. LET IT DRY AND IT WILL BECOME INVISIBLE. WHEN YOU'RE READY TO REVEAL THE MESSAGE, JUST HOLD THE PAGE UP TO A LIGHT BULB.

SCORES

109

120

121

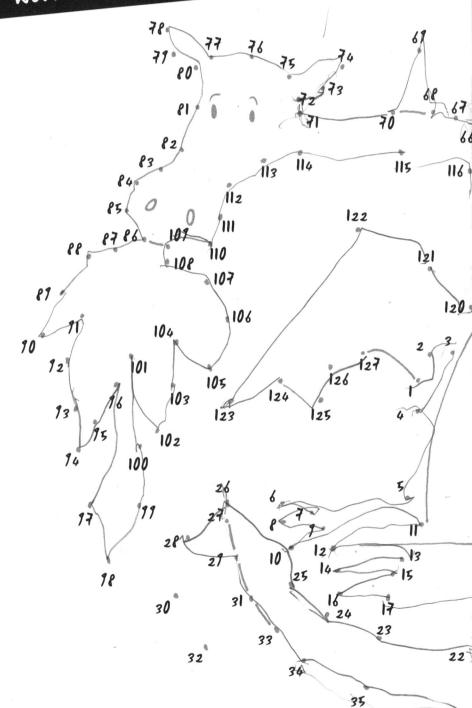

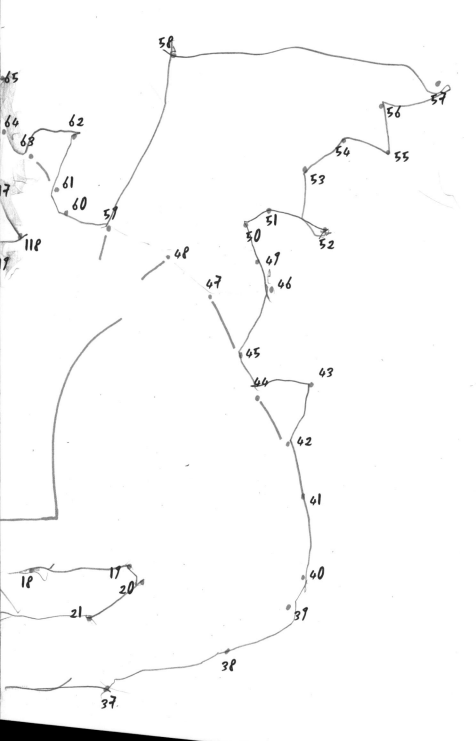

COLOR IN THEN CUT OUT PAGE 125
AND FOLD IT INTO A BOX. TELL YOUR
FRIENDS THAT YOU PUT SOMETHING DANGEROUS
INSIDE AND SEE IF THEY DARE TO OPEN IT.

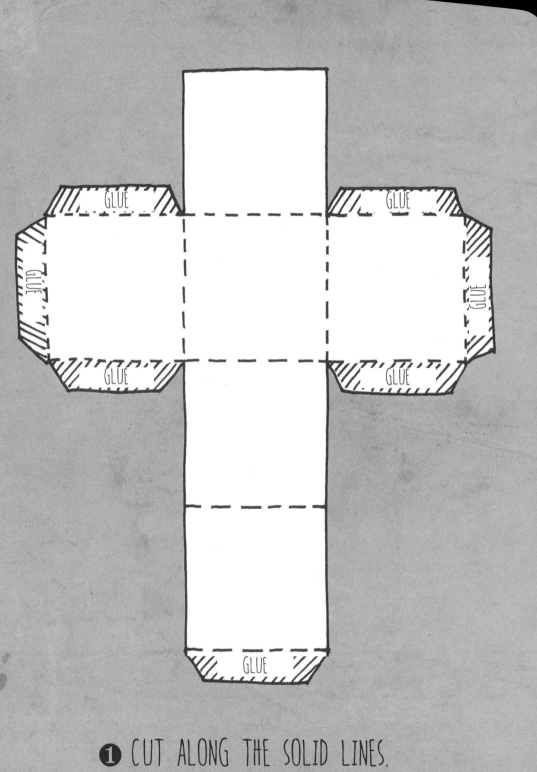

❶ CUT ALONG THE SOLID LINES.
❷ FOLD ALONG THE DOTTED LINES.
❸ GLUE THE SHADED AREAS.

CREATE A MAZE THAT DOESN'T HAVE AN

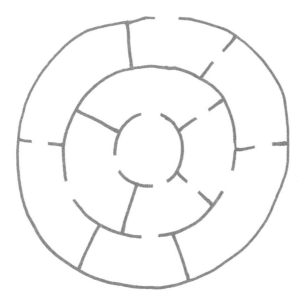

ENTRANCE OR AN EXIT. FILL BOTH PAGES.

WRITE THE DATE YOU BOUGHT OR RECEIVED
THIS KOOB IN MORSE CODE.

WRITE YOUR BIRTH DATE IN MORSE CODE.

WRITE THE ANSWER TO 74 + 22 + 11
IN MORSE CODE.

NUMBERS IN MORSE CODE:

STICK A COBWEB ON THESE PAGES.

MAKE YOUR OWN FLIP BOOK WITH A SCENE THAT WORKS BOTH FORWARDS AND BACKWARDS.

Instructions:

1) Cut out the squares on page 137.

2) Stack them on top of one another and fasten with a clip.

3) Draw a sequence of pictures, working from the top page to the bottom page.

4) Flip from top to bottom and then bottom to top to see your scene play forwards and backwards.

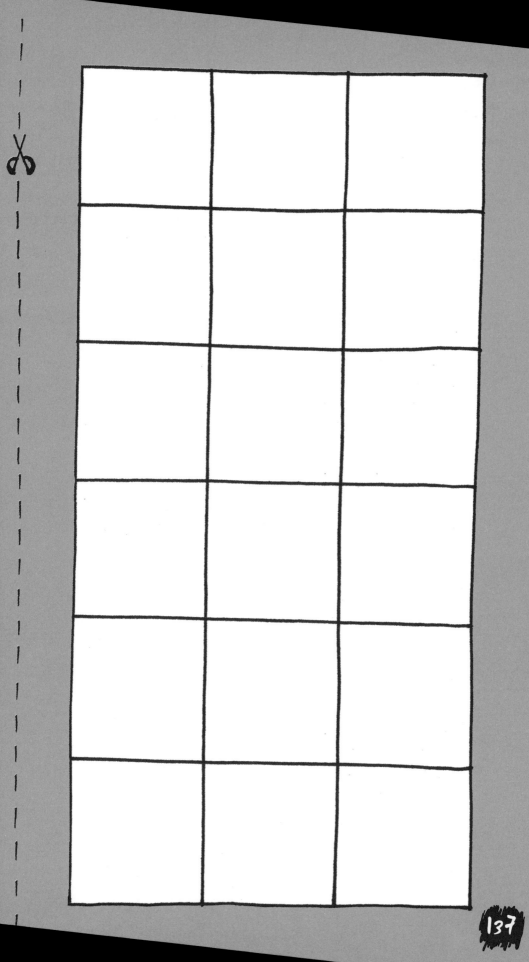

137

Cut out this page and swap it with your favorite page in the koob. Stick the pages back in with tape.

140

SPRAY THIS PAGE WITH PERFUME SO IT SMELLS NICE.

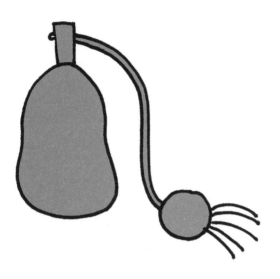

THIS IS A CARLTON KOOB.
TEXT, DESIGN, AND ILLUSTRATION © CARLTON BOOKS 2015

PUBLISHED IN 2015 BY CARLTON BOOKS LIMITED,
AN IMPRINT OF THE CARLTON PUBLISHING GROUP,
20 MORTIMER STREET, LONDON, WIT 3JW
THIS EDITION PUBLISHED IN THE UNITED STATES BY
SCHOLASTIC INC. JANUARY 2016
ALL RIGHTS RESERVED. SCHOLASTIC AND ASSOCIATED LOGOS
ARE TRADEMARKS AND/OR REGISTERED TRADEMARKS OF SCHOLASTIC INC.

10 9 8 7 6 5 4 3 2 1   16 17 18 19 20
ISBN: 978-0-545-90662-3

PRINTED AND BOUND IN CHINA

AUTHOR: TTERB ANNA
ILLUSTRATIONS: DRAW ELLE
DESIGN: ATSOC'AD EKAJ & LEXIP DLIW
OWNER OF KOOB: ....

BEST PAGE: ....

WORST PAGE: ....
FRIEND WHO YOU WANT TO
SHARE THIS KOOB WITH: ....

PICTURE CREDITS: SHUTTERSTOCK.COM

CONGRATULATIONS ON OPENING THIS KUOB!

EXPECTING PAGE 1?
NOT A CHANCE! IF YOU HAVEN'T ALREADY FIGURED IT OUT
FROM THE TITLE, KOOB IS A BACKWARDS BOOK, SO TURN
TO THE BACK AND FLIP IT UPSIDE DOWN TO GET STARTED.
THEN DOODLE, CUT, GLUE, FOLD, AND SCRIBBLE
YOUR WAY TO THE FRONT!